Changing LDS Messages for Blacks, Feminists, & Gays

(Note this conversation was recorded on July 3, 2020. The interview has been lightly edited for clarity.)

Introduction

Dr. Taylor Petrey discusses how rhetoric from LDS leaders about blacks, gays, and women has both accommodated and pushed back against American society's push for civil rights for these three groups. LDS discourse has changed markedly over the 20th century. We'll talk about his new book Tabernacles of Clay, and how much future change could follow past examples of change with regards to both race and feminism. In many cases, LDS leaders have accommodated changes while at the same time denouncing these movements. Check out our conversation….

Tags: Gospel Tangents, Rick Bennett, LDS Church, Latter-day Saints, LDS Church, Mormon, Mormon Church, Church of Jesus Christ of Latter-day Saints, Mormon history, Mormon, LDS Church, LDS, Church of Latter Day Saints, Taylor Petrey, Tabernacles of Clay, feminism, race ban, interracial marriage, marriage laws, LGBT, gays, lesbian, rhetoric, Phyllis Schlafly, ERA, women's rights, birth control, Equal Rights Amendment, Spencer Kimball, Barbara Smith, Dallin Oaks, apostle, BYU, same sex marriage, marriage, homosexuality, feminist, Mormon feminism, equal rights amendment, era, Mia Love, Peter Johnson, Gerrit Gong, birth control, lesbian, sexual fluidity

Contents

Introduction 2

LDS Leaders on Interracial Marriage 4

Feminism, Sexual Revolution, & LDS Church 15

Oaks' Role Designing LGBT Policy 23

Is Gay Contagious? 31

Additional Resources: 37

    Greg Prince on Gays & the Mormon Church...................37

    Anne Wilde on How Polygamist Feel About Gay Marriage.............38

    Bill Smith on Gay Marriage and D&C 132....................38

Final Note..39

LDS Leaders on Interracial Marriage

Introduction

I'm excited to introduce Dr. Taylor Petry, an associate professor at Kalamazoo College, and editor for the *Dialogue* Journal. In this first segment, we'll talk about how LDS leaders have changed how they talk about race issues, especially with regards to interracial marriage over the 20th century. Is this similar to possible changes regarding LGBT issues? Check out our conversation....

Interview

GT 00:05 All right. Welcome to *Gospel Tangents*. I'm excited to have an amazing Harvard-trained historian. I think you're my first. I don't think I've ever talked to anybody from Harvard. But could you go ahead and tell us who you are?

Taylor 01:19 Sure. I'm Dr. Taylor Petrey. I'm a professor at Kalamazoo College of Religious Studies. I got my graduate degrees at Harvard, so that's that backstory I guess. That's the basics.

GT 01:35 {In Boston accent} Did you paak ya caa at Haavaad Yaad?

Taylor 01:38 Many times, yes. I got lots of tickets, too.

GT 01:43 [Chuckling] I would like to get a little bit more of your background. I know your Ph.D. is a divinity degree or something like that?

Taylor 01:54 Yeah. So the Divinity School is one of the schools, like the law school and the medical schools, and so on, at Harvard. The Divinity School has been around for a couple of hundred years now. It was originally developed to train ministers, which it still does, but of course, it also has an academic mission as well. So that's

"

where the sort of seat of Religious Studies is at Harvard. So that's where my master's and doctoral degrees are both from.

GT 02:25 Oh, that's cool. So, you got your masters and doctorate there. Now, are you a Red Sox fan?

Taylor 02:31 You know, I went to lots of Red Sox games. But I stopped caring about sports a long time ago. So...

GT 02:39 Oh, that hurts my heart!

Taylor 02:40 I tried. I really... once I bought a TV and I was like, I'm going to get into sports and I'm going to care about sports. About a third of a way through a football game, I was like, this is as boring as I remember it was.

GT 02:53 {Chuckles} Well, Tom Brady--we can't talk about him. He's gone now. I haven't gotten on board. We've got Cam Newton now on the Patriots.

Taylor 03:03 It was fun living in Boston. I was there for a decade when they won the Stanley Cup, the World Series and the Super Bowl, just constantly during that decade, so there was always a party going on. It was a fun time.

GT 03:17 It was a great decade. It's been a great decade, and we can kiss 1918 goodbye.[1] So it's good. You know, 1918 was when they had that darn pandemic, too. This is my first remote interview. So I don't know if I like this, but we're going to try it anyway. So before that, did you go to BYU or anything? Where'd you get your bachelor's?

Taylor 03:40 I grew up in Utah, but I ended up going to New York City to Pace University for my undergraduate degree. I then went on

---

[1] After 1918, the Boston Red Sox did not win a World Series until 2004, the second longest drought of any team in baseball history.

a mission and came back and started studying religion there and just fell in love with the discipline and figured that this is what I want to do for the rest of my life.

GT 03:57 Oh, wow. That's awesome. What was your bachelor's degree in?

Taylor 04:00 Philosophy and religious studies.

GT 04:02 Oh, wow. So you're just all in, there. That's pretty cool. So Taylor, one of the interesting things about our relationship is we've teamed up with the *Dialogue Podcast Network*. So can you talk a little bit about your time as editor of *Dialogue* and how we teamed, how we got together, both of us?

Taylor 04:25 Yeah, I started the *Dialogue Podcast Network* not long after I became the editor of *Dialogue*, because I really wanted to get a number of great shows that were out there, like yours, into a kind of single collective where we could all promote and talk about each other's shows. So, the *Dialogue Podcast Network* emerged as sort of this group of thoughtful and interesting, diverse voices that were working in Mormon themed podcasting. I was really excited to have you join that, and work with us to work with all of these other shows that have such great things to say about Mormon history, about contemporary issues, about gospel doctrine, teachings and all kinds of different stuff. So, thanks for being a part of that.

GT 05:08 Yeah, well, it's been fun. So just for those of you who aren't familiar with it, it's kind of a lot like *Patreon*, in a way. It's more of towards educational sort of a thing. So the website is, is Lyceum. (I hate spelling it.) Lyceum.fm. You can subscribe to the *Dialogue Podcast Network*. So *Gospel Tangents* is in there. *Mormon News Report* is in there. The nice thing is--some of us only post once a week, I try to post about two or three times a week. So, if you're really into Mormon-themed podcasts, you can go to one place and you can get everybody and you don't have to wait a whole week for the next episode or, or three days or whatever it is. So It's updated quite a lot and it's been fun to be on there. How did you get hooked up with Lyceum? Can you tell that story?

Taylor 06:10 Yeah, one of our board members works with Lyceum and works in podcasting. So we really wanted to leverage the sort of resources that he had to offer us. It just seemed to be a great fit and a great platform for the kind of work that we did. [There are] a lot of great benefits for members who join with direct contact with the shows and with other early content, as you do, and sometimes there are some bonus episodes for other shows that only Subscribers get. So, it just seemed to have a lot of the features that we were looking for, and it was a great way to continue to create the community of podcast listeners that are out there.

GT 06:46 Yeah, so it's free to listen, I'll post my episodes there as well as on my podcast. But you'll also get *Mormon News Report* and *Beyond the Block* and some other things. Then, of course, *Dialogue*. I know you've had some Sunday School classes on there as well. So it's fantastic. That's awesome. Well, I've got your book here, Tabernacles of Clay,[2] there it is. I've read the whole thing. This is funny because I have to tell you, I think you hit all of the hot button topics, because you talk about blacks, feminists, and gays, and I'm like, wow, you kind of hit the trifecta there, didn't you?

Taylor 07:37 Sorry, I had to get my dog who is scratching at the door, rather than make him scratch the whole time. I figured I'd bring him in.

Taylor 07:45 Yeah, I wanted to bring those three things into conversation for a couple of reasons. First, that is sort of the broader trends of the field of what we call intersectionality, a sort of thinking about the interrelationship between these various categories of identity. Also, I was just seeing it in the sources themselves that these things were overlapping and that they

---

[2] Can be purchased at https://amzn.to/32bSKXY

needed to be put into conversation. Whereas we've had the history of race, we have LGBT histories, and we have the histories of women, I thought, we really need to tell these stories as a sort of single story. The same characters were involved in all of them, and the same logic in many cases is sort of working behind the scenes for the ways that church leaders are thinking about those issues. So, I wanted to kind of bring them all together. It's a sort of, 1-2-3 punch, there, a little bit. It's kind of hard sometimes.

GT 08:42 It really is. I have to tell you, sometimes it seems like when I talk about race issues, or if I talk about feminist issues, or if I talk about gay issues, people are like, why are you talking about this stuff? But I'm like, because it's fun to talk about and I like to talk about it and if you don't want to listen, you can skip this one. But I think these are all really important topics. I was really surprised because we've got the little rainbow here. I thought this was all going to be about, LGBT issues and it says *Sexuality and Gender in Modern Mormonism*, as your subtitle. So I was really pleasantly surprised, because I have to tell you, the priesthood ban and racial issues are one of my favorite topics. So it was really cool, because that's where you start out. So I'd love for you to kind of talk a little bit about the history of race in the LDS church and how that ties in with gay issues as well.

Taylor 08:59 Yeah. So the typical way that we have told the history of the priesthood ban has been primarily around focusing on race as the exclusive category. But when I started looking at the conversations that were happening and what church leaders were saying about race in the 1950s and 60s, I saw immediately that marriage was one of the big concerns. Why were they in favor of segregation? Why did they oppose civil rights? Why did they even have church policies that would prevent marriage in the temple?

Taylor: Because they were really concerned about interracial sex. They thought that this was a big, big problem. We have this whole ideology about race and racialized groups, that this group was destined to do this, and this group was destined to do that. They worried that interracial mixing would dilute the sort of divine designs for those particular races. So I immediately saw that the question of race was really entwined with the with questions of sexuality. Again, as a sort of modern parallel to issues around same sex relationships today, I also wanted to show that the question of 'who could marry who' wasn't just an issue that we dealt with in polygamy. It was an issue that we dealt with in the 1950s, 60s and 70s, and even up until the last decade, we still were publishing manuals that had quotes from Spencer W. Kimball discouraging interracial marriage.

Taylor 11:17 So the question of who can marry who, what kinds of couples are allowed in the church, in some cases, socially, and then in some cases ecclesiastically, was not just an old question, it was a pretty new question that we've dealt with. So I wanted to tell the history of how we worked through that particular issue as a way, not explicitly, but a parallel to the kinds of questions that we're dealing with [regarding] same sex relationships, too.

GT 11:49 Yeah, so it was great. I was really surprised to see how much detail you went into there. Can we talk a little bit more about some of the rhetoric around interracial marriage? What were some of the things said, and how are they similar to some of the things said today?

Taylor 12:05 Yeah. So, maybe there's something else that you're thinking of that if you want to prompt my memory about it, but one of the discourses that they were using was about purity. They were really thinking about racial purity as this value, as this good. Of course, that's rooted in white supremacist rhetoric and it's a based in some sort of hierarchical thinking as well--that some races were higher up on the hierarchy with respect to God. Of course, Latter-day Saints saw themselves as the best and the purest of all of those, right? We have this entire language about race that, for the most part, just doesn't exist today. I mean, if you look at something like the *Be One* campaign[3] that was done in 2018, in celebration of

---

[3] See https://www.youtube.com/watch?v=52-y98r2ZYs

the 40th anniversary of the priesthood revelation, you don't see appeals to the racialized groups of different people in their destinies. All that stuff is just totally gone. So both the kinds of purity and this discourse that races had a sort of divine design, that they were given by God these different tasks, and that comes out of U.S. Southern segregationist beliefs. So, of course, there were some Northerners that were segregationists, as well, and obviously, Latter-day Saints were. But this sort of segregationist thinking was also based on this idea that God created the races as discrete things, and that it was our obligation to sort of preserve those discrete boundaries between the races.

Taylor 13:46 So that language, then, of hierarchy, the language of purity, was also the same kind of language that they were using to talk about women's roles. It wasn't just about white supremacy, but also about patriarchy as well. So, during the same time period, we get a lot of the language of the patriarchal order of marriage. It's also a term that we just don't even hear anymore. But I grew up in the 90s, hearing this, I felt like, all the time, that there was such a thing as the patriarchal order of marriage. Now, you just won't find it in church manuals. That hasn't been spoken in general conference in a long, long time. So, the patriarchal order was also based on this notion of a sort of pure, discreet boundaries between the sexes, and that if we undertook activities that sort of blurred those boundaries or created instability between those boundaries, then we were also blurring God's will, just as we would be for the racial boundaries as well. So a lot of the same kinds of language, the same discourse about purity around boundaries, around a hierarchy. We see, as a kind of operating set of doctrinal underpinnings of a lot of the ways that church leaders were thinking about race, gender, and certainly sexuality, even today. We can make the same parallels about a hierarchy between hetero and homosexuality, the purity of boundaries between those, and so on, that kind of continues to influence the way that church leaders think about these things.

GT 15:13 Well, and it seems like marriage was a big issue, which is kind of funny. I don't know if violence is the right word, but the biggest opposition with Mormons in marriage--first we were polygamists. We were defending polygamy. Then the U.S. government beat that out of us. Then when it comes to race issues, interracial marriage, I know Petersen and McConkie and Joseph Fielding Smith had some real fire and brimstone kind of speeches about, we can't have interracial marriage. It's messing up God's plan. So it's interesting to me. I kind of want to tie this into feminism, because it ties into that, as well as in the gay marriage. It seems like Mormons are really trying to regulate marriage, that it's supposed to be whites only, or blacks only or Asians only. So, could you talk a little bit more about how Mormons are trying to define marriage? And if we do it wrong, it's going to bring the downfall of civilization.

Taylor 16:21 Yeah, we often end up on the wrong side of these issues, unfortunately, or at least in contemporary perspective, right. The kind of perspectives that we were defending a generation or two ago aren't necessarily the ones that we hold on anymore. But yeah, they had a whole theory that civilization was dependent on these hierarchies. There was a divinely imposed order of the races, of sexual hierarchy, as we mentioned, between men and women, and that, to our peril, we would undo all of those things and risk our own nation, and risk our own civilizational stability. You can understand this in the context of the Cold War, which is when many of these doctrines are really starting to be emphasized, and this rhetoric about national stability is showing up. Because we're seeing the same thing happening in evangelical and Protestant fundamentalist circles as well, this sort of emphasis on very rigid racial boundaries, and, of course, very rigid gender boundaries. These things get politicized later on with the religious right, which I'm sure we'll talk about at some point here.

Taylor: So Latter-day Saints sort of belonged to this broader culture in the ways that they're thinking about these civilizational risks in undoing these hierarchies, because the society is ordered a certain way and if you reordered it in the way that the people who are arguing for racial integration or the feminists were arguing for, then, of course, a certain group loses power and then it's going to be chaos and we're going to all fall to the communists or something like that. They looked to communism, specifically, which had feminist elements to it. Women would go to work and they would say, "Look how terrible that society is." Therefore, women going to work is a sign of communism. So you had all these sort of larger anxieties about gender roles. I wanted to also kind of place it in the context of a larger international story about the way that Latter-day Saints were thinking in nationalistic terms and American civilizational terms of sort of pro-democracy, pro-Western, in contrast to communism, at the time. They associated civil rights, they associated feminism with communism, and therefore, these were the things that were going to end America as we know it.

GT 18:59 Yeah. So I think what was interesting to me is, especially in the '50s, and 60s, that interracial marriage would bring about the downfall of civilization. Now we have a black general authority, which was unheard of in the 50s and 60s. Peter Johnson[4] is who I'm talking about, but he's married to a white woman. And we have an apostle, [Gerrit] Gong.[5] He's Asian, and he has a white wife as well. So, apparently, we've completely changed on this issue about whether interracial marriage is a good thing. I think you also mentioned Mia Love.[6] She's a black Congresswoman, and she has a white husband. So, talk about how we flip from, "This is the downfall of civilization," to totally embracing it now.

Taylor 19:57 Yeah. There was so much anxiety around it. It's almost hard to fathom how much anxiety there was, and it wasn't just black/white marriages that they were concerned about. Also, I go into talk a lot about the Native American, what was then called the Indian Placement Program, I believe.

GT 20:18 That's right.

---

[4] For more information, see https://www.churchofjesuschrist.org/learn/peter-m-johnson?lang=eng

[5] See https://www.churchofjesuschrist.org/learn/gerrit-w-gong?lang=eng

[6] See https://en.wikipedia.org/wiki/Mia_Love

Taylor 20:19 Where, especially Navajo children would be brought to northern Utah and other places and placed in white homes during the school year so that they could attend the public schools in the north. Then they would go back to the Navajo reservation, and other tribes were involved in this Indian placement program as well. Then what happens is people fall in love, and you get Native Americans and white people getting married and all of a sudden, the church starts freaking out about this. Spencer W. Kimball, who had been a big advocate of the Indian Placement Program, was out there as the biggest opponent of interracial marriage. The same thing happens when we're setting up BYU-Hawaii or whatever it was called back then, the Polynesian College.[7] I forget exactly what its name was back then. But, [you get the] same thing. You get social integration. That leads to marriages and relationships and the church is like, "Oh, this isn't what we meant. We wanted integration, but not intermarriage." So, there's a lot of anxiety about that. It's surprising that then, what are we 40-50 years later, now, General authorities who were those who were of that age when they were hearing all of these messages of: Don't get married, don't be involved in interracial marriages. They ignored that advice, got married anyway and now have become general authorities. So, I think that those are some really interesting ones.

Taylor 21:53 The Mia Love one I found particularly interesting because it's not just the racial boundaries that were being blurred in her case, but also she was, of course, working. She was a working mother and not only working in a high demand job, but a high demand job that often took her out of state, as well. Yet, the church didn't seem to have any problem with it. They promoted her on the *I'm a Mormon* campaign. There were newspaper articles in the *Deseret News*, talking about her and her relationship with her husband. So I wanted to sort of trace that shift. How do we get to today where these things aren't problematic, when they were [problematic] to the members of the 50s and 60s? If Joseph

---

[7] It was called Church College of Hawaii in 1955.

Fielding Smith were around today and saw what the makeup of the general authorities and the kinds of marriages that they were in, how many children they had, did they use birth control? All of those things he would be very confused by, because he was such a vehement opponent of those practices. So I wanted to understand, again, that these aren't--it's not just the change from monogamy to polygamy, that's not the only big change that we've made with respect to marriage and certainly not with respect to sexuality. It's much more recent than that, that we've been having this conversation inside of the church about who gets to marry who and what are the rules around that and so on.

Feminism, Sexual Revolution, & LDS Church

Introduction

Phyllis Schlafly was an important figure in defeating the Equal Rights Amendment, and she convinced LDS leaders to oppose the amendment. Dr. Taylor Petry will tell us more about how LDS messages have changed over the decades. Check out our conversation....

Interview

GT 23:25   Yeah, well, that's great. I think this is a good way to segue into chapter two, which deals with feminism. I'm probably old enough to barely remember Phyllis Schlafly. But I think a lot of my listeners are going to be like, "Now who's that?" But she was a very important figure. Can you introduce us to who is Phyllis Schlafly and why is she important?

Taylor 23:51   Yeah. If people haven't watched *Mrs. America* on Hulu, have you seen this yet, by the way?

GT 24:00   I don't have Hulu, so no, I haven't seen it.

Taylor 24:00   You've got to get Hulu. Anyway, it's one of the best shows. It's got an amazing cast and Phyllis Schlafly is the central character of the story and it tells the story. The book kind of gets into this a little bit, too. You've got feminism, which is, of course, on the rise in the 1960s and 70s. As often happens, there become, then, counter movements to oppose those things. Phyllis Schlafly becomes the most famous anti-feminist during this time period. Schlafly is a Catholic, and she sees something that had been happening in the broader conservative religious world at the time, where there had been a backlash to the kinds of feminism that was arising. But it hadn't really been organized as a political movement. So she sees that evangelicals and Protestant fundamentalists and even Mormons, are opposing feminism. She says we need to unite all of these people into a single coalition that will be able to speak for our values. The big issue of the time period is the Equal Rights Amendment. The Equal Rights Amendment was hugely popular among Democrats and Republicans.

Taylor: All the Republicans at the outset of it passing in Congress, were ecstatic about it, and then it needs to march through the states. Immediately it's passed by the first 32 states within the first year or something like that. That's when the opposition really gets going. When the *Stop ERA* movement that Phyllis Schlafly is organizing and pulling together--all the sort of anti-feminist groups into a political coalition and the Church gets involved. [The Church] is specifically recruited by Phyllis Schlafly to get involved in this fight. [The Church] politically mobilizes, for the first time in decades at that point. The Church had not really seen itself as having a political mission. Even during ERA, at the very beginning, if you asked church leaders in the first couple of years that the ERA was a public topic, in the early 70s--the ERA had been around since the 1920s. But it really kind of gets going in the early 70s. It was supposed to be the sort of follow-up to the civil rights amendments or civil rights movements of the 1960s. So now it's the feminists turn, so the Church gets recruited to do this and reverses itself because at first it was a no, this is a political issue. We don't comment on political issues. We just care about moral issues, not political ones. But Phyllis Schlafly convinces the church that this is a moral issue, that it's not just a political issue. So the Church decides to mobilize its membership in this political fight, and they start sending members to ERA conventions to shout down the leaders that are there, and to disrupt the meetings. The Church's, nearly decade long, it lasted about eight years, fight against the Equal Rights Amendment until it was finally defeated in 1982, decisively. This was one of the major ways that the church gets involved in the anti-feminist movement. So yeah, that's the that's the basic history of who Schlafly is and how she kind of gets the church involved in this.

Taylor 25:22 It was interesting to me to hear how she recruited LDS members, because it seems like she went first to the General Relief Society president, then that kind of morphed into President Kimball. Could you give us a few more details on that? That was really surprising to me. I didn't know any of that history. That was awesome.

Taylor 27:45 Yes. So she secures a meeting with Barbara B. Smith, who was brand new in her role as Relief Society president and had just taken over from Elouise Bell, I think, is who it was before. I might be misremembering that, but she had been the Relief Society president for over 20 years, was a very well-known popular figure, a nationally known figure in some cases, because she was involved in a number of national women's organizations. So Barbara B. Smith, I think she had just been in the job a few months when she takes this meeting with Schlafly, and then [Barbara B.] Smith takes it to the male general authorities, to the Apostles, and they say, maybe this is a good idea, and they organize a meeting for her to come out and speak publicly.

Taylor 28:34 Because the politics of having women oppose the Equal Rights Amendment, were very powerful. That's why Schlafly was so successful. If men were out there opposing the Equal Rights Amendment, it just looked like old-fashioned patriarchy. But if you get women involved in anti-feminism, then it's going to be much more successful. So they initially have Barbara B. Smith as sort of being the public face of the Church's opposition, but soon the male church leaders really take the lead after that, and start to call the shots and run a whole political playbook and so on. It's a political playbook that works really, really well. It's extremely effective. It gets a lot of attention from Schlafly, from the other members of the religious right and it's one that they then use in later political battles against same sex marriage as well. They have a whole set of tools and strategies. Many of the people who were running the opposition to the Equal Rights Amendment including Hinckley, Monson, these guys then become the leaders of the Church's opposition to same sex marriage in the 1990s and 2000s. They are running some of the same plays that they used then, as well. So, they learned a lot from it, in terms of having a successful campaign. If you look at it, they were very successful. They defeated the ERA, and it's not looking like it's going to come back. I mean, there are some rumblings every once in a while, it's going to come back.

Taylor: So you can see why they thought, "This was wildly successful." We won not only the political, but also the cultural battle against it, and it's not coming back. So, when they finally do get to same sex marriage, I'm jumping ahead a little bit here, right, but just trying to play this up. When they do get to same sex marriage, they think, "Oh, we can be just as successful, if not more, on this as we were in opposing feminism." That turns out to be a miscalculation. So that's a little bit of how they get involved in this issue and how they change from just preaching anti-feminist values, in favor of the patriarchal order, to then making it into a whole political strategy, too.

GT 30:43 It was interesting, also, to see how the church changed from this patriarchal order of marriage, into a more of an egalitarian [order], It's almost as if they adopted a lot of the ERA words and things. But yet they were still anti-feminist. Can you talk about how that evolved, that change in rhetoric in the LDS leaders?

Taylor 31:09 Yeah, so I try to chart a split in the way that Church leaders start to think about feminist issues, in their opposition to the Equal Rights Amendment. While we only really heard the patriarchal order in the 50s, and 60s, when we get to the 70s, and definitely in the 80s, we start to see, certainly, the patriarchal order continues. There are a number of strong proponents of the patriarchal order, but we start to see another branch of LDS thought developing. We're finding it in LDS feminists from this time period as well. But we're definitely even seeing it among general authorities who are taking a much softer stance on the patriarchal order and are much more open to egalitarian marriage, which was the sort of ideal of marriage that many feminists and certainly Mormon feminists were advocating: the idea that male and female, the husband and wife are equal partners in the relationship.

Taylor 32:05 So we see this kind of split, this tension between the two. Kimball on the one hand and Benson certainly. Benson is probably the most famous example of the sort of patriarchal order that lasts up through the 80s, while you've got Barbara Smith and Hinckley and a few others who are trying to take a little bit softer and more accommodationist stance. [They] want to say, "We don't oppose equal rights for women. We don't oppose the equality between men and women. We actually support it. We just don't think that the Equal Rights Amendment is the best way to do that." So, they want to support the cause, but not support the specific policy, while others don't want to support the cause or the policy at all. So you see a kind of new way of thinking about relationships as possibly egalitarian and the egalitarian relationships may be compatible with Mormon teachings emerging in this time period, and, of course, today, I think egalitarianism is pretty much the dominant strain within marriage, right?

Taylor 33:10 It's pretty much the dominant strain the way that we think about it. But even if you look at something like the Proclamation on the Family[8] that comes about in 1995, you see the ways in which that reflects that internal tension between egalitarianism on the one hand, because it has husband and wife are equal partners. Then also, at the same time, you have the patriarchal language of, the husband presides. How can you have husband presides and that they're equal partners? That doesn't make any sense, right? But we have this tension that is these two different streams of the way that the church is thinking about its teachings to widen itself in such a way to be able to accommodate both--so that both sides of this issue can be happy, and it sort of helps to defuse some of the feminist critiques that were happening.

---

[8] See https://www.churchofjesuschrist.org/study/scriptures/the-family-a-proclamation-to-the-world/the-family-a-proclamation-to-the-world?lang=eng

Taylor 33:10 Of course, the question of priesthood and the question of church leadership is a separate one. So I'm confining myself here to the question of marriage, itself. But at least in that sphere, they tend to be much more accommodating and open to new kinds of relationships. Of course, also, because that's what church members were doing. Church members were having egalitarian relationships and young women who had grown up in a feminist era, even if they weren't feminists, just expected a sort of different kind of freedoms than their mothers may have had, and different kinds of opportunities than their mothers may have had. So, part of the reason I think we are also seeing the shift in church teachings is because that's how members are actually practicing it at that point, too.

GT 34:48 The other interesting thing I think about ERA, is they were worried about how that would affect lesbians and also how birth control was kind of a big issue about whether you should even use it. Can you talk a little bit about how the church kind of evolved with birth control, especially? That was an interesting movement.

Taylor 35:13 Yeah, let me talk about the ERA and same sex attraction and homosexuality. Because I think that one of the things that many people miss, they see that as an anti-feminist action. But what the church is doing in its opposition to the Equal Rights Amendment is that they're very explicitly linking feminism to homosexuality. They even say in the documents that they are distributing to church members, that this is going to lead to same sex marriages and even worse, same sex couples might be raising children, and freaking out about that. Then they are saying things like, "If a woman goes to work and even dresses like a man," I mean, at this point, they're still worried about women wearing pants instead of skirts. That's where they are. That's where they're at. "Then they're going to become man-ish in their desires, and they're going to be attracted to women."

Taylor 36:15 It's not quite how it works, actually. But that's what really what they're thinking is that if you behave and if you act like a man, then you're going to desire women. That's where we get lesbians. That's how lesbians come about. So, they're linking and they're seeing sort of women's liberation and homosexuality as joint issues. In order to fight one, you have to fight the other. So they see them as linked, which again, is why I think some of the histories that have come up before this that don't connect LGBT history in the church and anti-feminist history in the church, have fully grasped the way that the church leaders, at least, saw those as integrated.

Taylor 36:59 The question of birth control is an interesting one. Because there was really almost no accommodation to birth control. The church was very strongly opposed to it. They saw it as what they called an unholy and impure practice. They warned that people were going to be denied celestial blessings, if they ever practiced birth control. That, I think, included even what we would call natural methods. They didn't want anything that limited output in any way. There were people who were pushing back against this even in the 1960s. Hugh B. Brown, the sort of liberal member of the First Presidency, thought that couples should be able to make their own decisions. So, we have some opposition to the anti-birth control movement within the church, but the dominant form in the Church up until the 1980s had been really to discourage it, highly discourage it.

Taylor 37:57 Then we got a policy change in 1983 that says it's up to the couple, and we're not going to pry about it, and you guys just make your own decisions. But this was a huge controversy in the church. It was, again, in the broader society as well, in the 1960s, you have the introduction of the pill as the first widely publicly available form of birth control. It was hugely popular as a result. It's one of the things that helps to fuel the sexual revolution of the 1960s and 70s. That's part of the reason why church leaders were also really skeptical of it. Again, they connected birth control and illicit sex as one leads to the other.

GT 38:38 It leads to the ERA as well, right?

Taylor 38:39 Yeah. Exactly. So church members are often, not always, but are often just ignoring those teachings, and so I think that's another reason why we see the church leadership change its policies, from what we would call a sort of pro-creationist or pronatalist sexual ethics. The purpose of sex was for reproduction. That's the way that church leaders thought about it. But you get in the 70s and then in the 80s, the kind of softening of that, where they say, "Well, that's one of the purposes, but another purpose is spousal bonding, happiness, enjoyment and those kinds of things." So, once they start to sort of acknowledge that that's not the exclusive purpose for sexual intimacy between couples, and they relax the teachings on birth control. With that comes a total change in the way that we think about sexuality in the church. Sex isn't just exclusively for reproduction. It takes on all of these other meanings. So there is really kind of a mini sexual revolution in the church during this time period as a result.

Oaks' Role Designing LGBT Policy

Introduction

In our next conversation with Dr. Taylor Petrey, we'll talk about Elder Oaks' pivotal role in outlining strategy for preventing acceptance, and some accommodation, or gay rights and gay marriage. We'll also talk about the internet rumor that the Family Proclamation was a result of the court case in Hawaii in the 1990s. Check out our conversation….

Interview

GT 39:48 Yeah. Well, it's interesting. I think you've really laid the foundation well with talking about interracial marriage and then talking about feminism. So that leads to gay rights and that sort of thing. This is one thing, I don't think this was in your book, but it's a question that I've had come up a lot. I really want to talk about it because we talked a little bit about it with Greg Prince.[9] There's an internet rumor, basically, that says that the *Proclamation on the Family* was a response to what was going on with gay marriage in Hawaii in about 1995, I believe it was.

GT 40:33 As we talk about kind of the history of gay rights and that sort of thing, can you address that issue? I've even heard the rumor that the *Proclamation on the Family* was not written by the apostles. It was written by the Kirton & McConkie law firm. Can you enlighten us on that? Is that a true story?

Taylor 40:53 It may be. It may be, but the documents don't fully support at least one iteration of that internet rumor. So let me sort of lay out the timeline a little bit, because I do think it's important. I

____

[9] See our interview at https://gospeltangents.com/2019/06/mixing-church-politics-lgbt-fight/

absolutely do think that the *Proclamation on the Family* is connected to what was going on in Hawaii and is connected to a broader set of conversations. So I do mention some of this in the book. But let me get into a little bit of the detail here.

GT 41:23 You don't get into the conspiracy, though, right?

Taylor 41:26 I don't explicitly address it. I say what I think the documents will support. So one iteration of the rumor is that it was needed in order for the church to win a certain set of legal battles that they were engaged in, in the courts there. I don't think that that's accurate. I don't think that that's an accurate understanding of what was happening. But it's in 1993, that Hawaii's Supreme Court legalized same sex marriage, but they put a stay on the decision. Meaning that they say it's not going to go into effect. We're going to hear another round of arguments. This other round of arguments will try to establish whether or not there really are compelling reasons why the state needs to discriminate on the basis of sex when it comes to marriage.

Taylor 42:20 So same sex marriage is technically legal, but not able to be put into practice yet because they're waiting for the sort of other sets of arguments. So, what happens is that Hawaii's conservative church leaders and so on, and, of course, the LDS Church is getting involved in this, start to make a campaign against same sex marriage in Hawaii. They are appointed to a commission. First, there's Catholics and LDS people are appointed to a commission that's going to study the issue and the commission is then that report is then going to go to the courts for the courts to evaluate it. But the commission itself is disbanded as unconstitutional because it's mixing church and state. It has all of these [problems.] They're appointed specifically as LDS and Catholic representatives on this [commission] for their religious affiliations, to write these opinions. The Supreme Court says, "No, no, no, no. You don't get to have a state appointed theological commission here."

Taylor 43:22   So they disband the commission, and then that really freaks out the LDS church. This happens, I think, in 1994, maybe 1995 or early 1995. So, the church is really feeling like they're going to lose this battle. The Supreme Court there is not open to their arguments. They're getting shut out at every step along the way. So, two things happen. In Utah, the Church really seems to be behind the scenes in passing a defense of marriage act, which says that if same sex marriage is legalized in Hawaii, we're not going to recognize it here in Utah, and that then becomes the basis for a whole...everybody else, right after Utah adopts a Defense of Marriage Act, that says the same thing: wherever same sex marriage is legal, if it happens to become legal in one state, it's not going to be legal here. Then the Clinton administration signs a federal Defense of Marriage Act, as well, which says the same thing. The federal government will not recognize same sex relations, same sex marriages that happened in any particular state. This is because they think that same sex marriage is going to happen in Hawaii. They're pretty sure at this point.

GT 44:43   The reason why is because if you don't have a law, and I'm not a constitutional scholar, but isn't there some sort of a constitutional argument that if something's recognized in one state, it has to be recognized in all states, unless that state has a law, and so that's why these laws all of a sudden go crazy.

Taylor 45:02   Yes. The constitutionality of those laws was precisely always in question, and they eventually lose, when the issue goes before the Supreme Court in 2015. The federal government at the time refuses to defend these Defense of Marriage Act laws because they say they're not constitutional. We agree with the opposition. These are not constitutional. The same thing had happened with interracial marriage, too. It's like, "Okay, well, in Virginia, interracial marriage is illegal, even though they were married in another state." This was the Loving versus Virginia decision in 1967.[10] So, the same constitutional issues were just replaying themselves here, that

---

[10] For more information, see https://en.wikipedia.org/wiki/Loving_v._Virginia

we're not going to recognize some marriages that are performed legally and lawfully in another state.

Taylor 45:49 So the church comes out with a proclamation. It's an affirmation of a kind of theological vision, that marriage is between a man and a woman, and it's an explicitly political document. At the end, the last paragraph says, "We appeal to citizens and judges, and we appeal to legislatures and leaders all throughout the world…" that this is the thing that you need to make sure that basically that same sex marriage doesn't happen. Same sex marriage and homosexuality aren't mentioned in the document. But it's absolutely the implicit thing, because the church is deeply embedded in what's going on in Hawaii. Did they need to do that for some sort of legal tricky reasons? I don't think so. But it becomes a kind of clarion call, a kind of thing that unites the church membership and says, this is our political stance. And again, we have to read it as a political document.

Taylor 46:45 The other part of the context that I think needs to be understood, is that there are a number of political documents that are coming out during this exact same time period, both before and after the LDS version of the *Proclamation*, that are making the exact same kinds of arguments. So, Phyllis Schlafly ran something called the Eagle Forum. She was still alive, at the time, in the 1990s. She passed away, I think, maybe five or so years ago. But she was running the Eagle Forum. Then there were other conservative groups, and they all got together, and they wrote a document in 1993, I want to say, maybe it was 1989. Again, my memory is fuzzy a little bit here, called The Family Manifesto.[11] *The Family Manifesto* looks exactly like what the *Proclamation on the Family* does, except it's longer. I think it's five pages or so. It says, what are the obligations of husbands and wives to each other? What are the obligations of husbands and wives to their children? What are the basic scriptural values that inform these positions?

---

[11] See https://www.familylife.com/aboutus/the-family-manifesto/

Taylor 47:54 It took a little bit more aggressive stances on issues like spousal hierarchy than the LDS version does, but it does affirm their equal dignity. Husband and wife have equal dignity before God, it says. So we still have some of that egalitarian and patriarchal tension even in a document like that. Then after that, there are other documents that look very similar to the LDS version of the *Proclamation*. So I also want to put the *Proclamation* in the context of all of these other political documents that the religious right is producing, that is sort of laying out an anti-feminist and anti-homosexuality agenda as a political thing. And again, [we should] understand the *Proclamation* as a political document, and to see it in conversation with all of those. Did Kirton & McConkie write it? I've heard that rumor, too. I don't know. Probably they were consulted on it in some way, as many public documents are consulted with the legal teams, of course. Every institution does that. They may even have had researchers that were looking at some of these other...

Taylor 49:00 The similarities between the Proclamation and some of these other conservative documents are so striking to me, at least, that it would be surprising to me if they didn't know them, if they didn't have them in front of them, because the order, the organization, the topics that are addressed, and even in some cases, the wording is so similar. They seem to really be relying on [each other.] They're a part of a genre, at least. The LDS *Proclamation* is part of a genre of these other documents coming out of the religious right during the 90s.

GT 49:18 I'm going to get these mixed up. So the LDS *Family Proclamation*, was that before the family manifesto of the evangelicals? [Taylor shakes his head.] No. Was it the other way around?

Taylor 49:35 Yes.

GT 49:42 Okay, so the *Proclamation* copies the *Family Manifesto*. Okay.

Taylor 49:48 Yes, copies is a strong word. It seems to be influenced by, or at least--I don't know if they, I would be surprised if they didn't have it in front of them, myself, because of those strong similarities, but I can't say for certain that it was consulted. There are no footnotes, and I haven't been able to talk to anybody who was in the room in the drafting of it, who may have known what sources were used as they looked into this. But there are a lot of [similarities.] One can read the *Family Manifesto*, this Catholic/Evangelical iteration, and very quickly see resonances in the LDS version.

GT 50:20 Oh, that's very interesting. So the other thing that I found really super interesting about that chapter was that Elder Dallin Oaks seems to be the point man for gay issues specifically. It seemed like you really...I want to ask this question. Do you think that's why he was called to be an apostle was because of his legal background and they were worried that, as ERA was passed that it would lead to gay marriage and that sort of a thing?

Taylor 51:08 Possibly. They had already won the ERA battle by the time that Oaks comes on in leadership, though Oaks had been president of BYU before that. There is also often a pipeline that we see. Holland, Eyring and others, people who've been presidents of one of the Church's schools are often then taken into the more senior leadership. So there are a variety of qualifications that I'm sure that he has, but his legal expertise and his reputation outside of the church--he was a University of Chicago law professor. He had argued in front of the Supreme Court on a number of occasions. He had been on the Utah Supreme Court. His resume is unparalleled, honestly. So he has lots of qualifications. But one of the first things that he does, at least as we can near as we can tell just based on the timeline of things, is issue what's called a white paper, a memorandum, to his colleagues that has since leaked out. I'm not the first one to talk about it. Lots of people have talked about it, so I feel comfortable, the fact that it's a public document now, even though it was not intended originally. [It was] for private use. [I] need to talk about it as a historian. But it lays out a strategy of how the church is going to be dealing with gay rights going forward. He sees on the horizon that this is going to be the big issue. Feminism, they won. We won that. We beat ERA.

Taylor 52:35 How are we going to then be really smart and strategic in opposing gay rights? Oaks had replaced Mark E. Peterson, and Mark E. Peterson was really quite conservative on gay rights issues. He was a big opponent of legalizing sodomy. So, there were a bunch of anti-sodomy laws that were being repealed in the 1970s. Mark E. Peterson was out there saying, "No, no, no. We need to keep these and this is disgusting and..." This is, again, "Our civilization is going to crumble if we legalize sodomy." Elder Oaks comes on and takes a totally different tack. He says, "Listen, sodomy, we're not going to get involved in this anymore. It's going to be legal. These are consenting adults." Basically, he's like, that's not the issue. He says, even employment discrimination with certain exceptions, we're not going to get involved in that. We're not going to say that gay people can't work anymore. He carves out some exceptions and says, maybe not in schools. We're not going to allow them to work in schools, but we're not going to get involved in this. Where we need to save our energy is for the coming battle on same sex marriage and he writes this in 1984, nine years before the Hawaii Supreme Court legalized same sex marriage. But he anticipates that this is going to be the thing. The reason why is because same sex marriage had been on the agenda in the 70s and 80s, among gay rights activists as well. So again, it wasn't invented in the 1990s. It wasn't invented in the 2000s. People were talking about this back in the 60s and 70s, and definitely in the 80s. Oaks sees. If we're going to get involved in opposing gay rights, we need to maintain some credibility on this issue and save it for gay marriage. That's the one thing that we really need to care about. Because if gay marriage is legalized, then it becomes socially normal to such an extent that we won't be able to teach against it anymore. So he really anticipates exactly where we are today. You know, that...

GT 54:51 Is it prophetic?

Taylor 54:53 Probably. Yeah. He would say so, I'm sure. He has all of the same arguments; arguments that he doesn't seem to hold today anymore, but sort of. He warns about homosexual recruitment in this document. I think his views have changed over time. I don't want to say that what he said in 1984 is probably exactly what he thinks today. But he definitely seems to have thought a lot about this issue in anticipation of what is going to come and seems to be one of the most important figures in the church's positions on homosexuality and same sex marriage, certainly since he became an apostle, and continues to this day to be one of the leading speakers on this topic.

GT 55:43 Would you say that Oaks, Hinckley and Monson were probably the three ringleaders, for lack of a better word, as far as opposition to both feminism and gay marriage.

Taylor 55:59 I think Maxwell is probably in the mix a little bit. There are some people who know all the dirt and the secrets and the rumors and stuff like that and I'm not one of those people. I had to rely on the public documents to tell this story. But I think Maxwell is in the mix. Obviously, Packer is also. Packer is a big player in this. He's one of the major vocal opponents to the Equal Rights Amendment. Some of the worst things that were said about the Equal Rights Amendment by Church leaders were said by Packer. He was in strongly in the patriarchal camp of things. He's also one of the most outspoken teachers, up until his death, opposing homosexuality. Again, some of the "worst" things that were ever said by church leaders in the modern era, were said by Elder Packer. So I think we have to put him in that category as one of the main drivers in the Quorum of the Twelve, at least on these issues.

GT 57:02 Cool.

Is Gay Contagious?

Introduction

In our next conversation, we'll talk about whether homosexuality, and heterosexuality, are contagious. Is it possible to change one's sexual attraction? Dr. Taylor Petrey will talk about how LDS Church leaders' views have changed over the past half century.

Interview

GT 57:03 So, a couple other issues that I thought were really interesting from your book was this whole idea of sexual fluidity. So I'm going to ask the question this way. Is gay contagious? Maybe I should say it this way. Do church leaders think gay is contagious?

Taylor 57:29 Great question. The answer is that up until very recently, yes. And they thought that heterosexuality was contagious, too. So the whole idea behind the notion of a gay cure, which is what people like Packer and others were promising, and we invested a ton of resources, both intellectual and material resources into the idea of a cure that would be helped by things like reparative therapy, and so on. The idea was, well, if we can teach these men, and most of the concern is around men, which I want to acknowledge. Lesbians do sort of fall in the background a little bit. When they're talking about feminism, they're talking about lesbians, but when they're talking about homosexuality, they're talking about men. They say, "Listen, we can teach these guys to play some sports, give them some confidence in basketball. If we can teach these guys to work on a car, or take up these manly activities and be around other manly men, who know how to do this stuff, then they're going to be just fine and their desires are going to become heterosexual. It was the same way that the worry of the working woman was going to start to desire sexually other women. The concern was that the reason why men were gay is that they hadn't appropriated masculinity enough. So that's why these issues of

31

gender and sexuality, are so closely connected for church leaders because they see heterosexuality as the proper outcome of masculinity, or the proper outcome of femininity. When masculinity and femininity themselves are being weakened in some ways, when suddenly women can now work, and be doctors and lawyers, and maybe men might be staying home or maybe men are sharing leadership with their wives in the home, then masculinity is going to be weakened to such an extent that if it doesn't cause homosexuality for the equal father himself, who's equal with his wife, it's going to cause it in his children.

Taylor 59:35 So his children are going, his male children are going to desire in abnormal ways, right? So this notion of sexual fluidity is really kind of the basis of the way that church leaders are thinking about heterosexuality and homosexuality as sort of, "If you can become one you can also become the other." Why they're worried about the normalization of homosexuality, then, during this period, is because it's contagious. They say, numerous times, including Dallin Oaks in that document that we were just talking about in 1984, that if homosexuality is socially normal, then within one generation, everyone will become gay, and then the population will die out.

GT 1:00:22 Didn't they make the same argument about interracial marriage?

Taylor 1:00:26 Well, not necessarily the population would die out, but they made the same argument that, look, homosexual sex must be so good, that it's going to be so attractive to people, that everyone's going to want to do it. If we don't have some sort of negative stigmas against it, then everyone would be gay. That leads to this idea, then, that they don't believe that people are naturally heterosexual. They don't believe there's some sort of hard wiring. They think that the only way that you become heterosexual is through this sort of molding and shaping of the human being into the properly formed masculine or properly formed feminine person. So it requires a lot of work on behalf of society, on behalf of the Church, on behalf of families, to kind of produce heterosexuality.

GT 1:01:16 Well, I will just mention my interview with Russell Stevenson,[12] we talked more about 19th century race, but there was, especially in the 19th century, it was scientifically known that mulattos or sometimes they would call them half breeds, (obviously, we wouldn't use that term today,) would become sterile. So that would be the end of civilization if white people married black people, that it was the end of civilization. So I'm hearing echoes, a lot of this end of the civilization, if we allow gay marriage, if we allow interracial marriage. So, it's funny to me, this end of civilization, I mean, it's very--what's the word? It's a fear-based argument that, if we do this, we're going to have moral decline, civilization is going to end, end of the Roman Empire. Even with polygamy, they use some of those same terms. Rome ended because they weren't polygamous, they were monogamous. So it's funny to me how these arguments get repeated over and over. They're just silly arguments, aren't they?

Taylor 1:02:29 There's a kind of, a sort of moral panic discourse about any change. The reason why our civilization is so great is because we've embraced these values, right? So progressive values that call into question those established ones, are then obviously going to be undoing all of the greatness that we've done, right? So you see this exact same tension in the sort of progressive and conservative debates about society, about morals, about policing right now. We're seeing this conversation. Certainly about sexuality, it's always been there. Yes, so you're absolutely right. I hope that one of the things that this book does is give a little bit of context to where those arguments come from and how they were formed. Because they're citing sources. They have arguments and I try to explain where those arguments are coming from and why they were so popular among church leaders during the time.

---

[12] See https://gospeltangents.com/2018/02/brigham-changed-mind-black-ordination/

GT 1:03:30   Yes. Interesting. All right. Well, the last topic I just wanted to cover with you really quickly was the church's dual kind of embracing gays, I mean the Mormon and Gay website,[13] but yet opposing it at the same time. Can you talk about how the Church kind of, I don't know, I don't want to say schizophrenic, but it was kind of weird how there were kind of two tracks going at the same time.

Taylor 1:04:00   Yes, so just like we see this sort of split in the egalitarian and patriarchal marriage ideas, we also are seeing a split in the church leadership over the nature of sexuality. How "contagious" is it? For instance, there's a number of church leaders who, I think, are starting to, in the early 2000s are started to kind of back away from reparative therapy, maybe trying to take a little bit more open and accommodating and even affirming stances. So it's in 2007, that BYU changes its policy that says that it's okay to identify as gay. At BYU, before you weren't allowed to do that. The way that the policy was often interpreted was, if you identified as gay, you were violating church doctrine on that topic, on that subject, and that was because of things that Elder Oaks, himself, specifically had said that you weren't allowed to do that and be a member, basically in good standing. It was against doctrine to say that.

Taylor 1:05:00   So then we start to see the softening, really again, in response to the backlash from Prop 8. So, 2008 comes along and we see the church sort of say, "We've got a real problem here that many of our church members have very negative attitudes towards gay and lesbian members of the Church." A number of activists work very hard, I think, to get the church to sort of see this as a problem that it needed to address. So we get, in the early 2010s, Mormons and Gays, and then later Mormon and Gay, I think came out in 2016, where the church is really trying to trying to address this issue and take a little bit of a softer stance. The church is going to allow for members to identify as gay and lesbian, and not be under

---

[13] See https://www.churchofjesuschrist.org/topics/gay/

social sanction or ecclesiastical sanction for that. They encourage the broader membership of the church to be loving and accepting towards those who do identify, which is quite different from what they were doing even a decade before that, which was discouraging people from identifying, telling families that they shouldn't accept their gay and lesbian children in their homes if they had a partner and so on. So, we really see the church backing away from some of the harsher things that it was saying, and attempting to accommodate same sex or gay and lesbian members of the church up until the point of having a relationship. So that becomes the sort of bright line there that the Church won't own. It won't tolerate that. So it opens itself up to saying that certain identities are acceptable within the Church, while certain practices are still forbidden. So it takes a sort of identity versus practice distinction, there.

GT 1:06:55 Yes. Well, great. Well everybody, *Tabernacles of Clay*. You should definitely get it. It is a fantastic book. I really appreciate you spending some time here. Is there anything that we've missed or anything that we you'd like to share with us before I let you go?

Taylor 1:07:12 Oh, good question. I've been talking so much. Let me think if I if there was anything else, I think that's probably some of the main things. So yeah.

GT 1:07:21 Well, fantastic.

Taylor 1:07:23 Oh, there was. I wanted to thank you for all the work that you do. This is such a great podcast, such a great show, and thanks so much for having me.

GT 1:07:32 Oh, well, no problem. So all right. Well, you know what? I think I might be giving away a copy of this. I wish I could get you to autograph it. That would be really cool. But if we have these conferences next year, maybe you'll get one of these. It'll be a gift from me, as well. So Dr. Taylor Petrey. Thank you so much for participating here on *Gospel Tangents*, I really appreciate it.

Taylor 1:07:57 It was a pleasure.

Additional Resources:

Greg Prince on Gays & the Mormon Church

Dr. Greg Prince details the history of LDS political fights over gay marriage from the 1990s through today.

286: Legal & Science Issues on LGBT
https://gospeltangents.com/2019/06/legal-science-social-lgbt/

285: Revelatory Whiplash
https://gospeltangents.com/2019/06/revelatory-whiplash/

284: The Christian Right & LGBT Fight
https://gospeltangents.com/2019/06/christian-right-lgbt-fight/

283: Mixing Church & Politics in Gay Fight
https://gospeltangents.com/2019/06/mixing-church-politics-lgbt-fight/

094: "There is Nothing in LDS Theology that Justifies Whacking Infants" (POX)
https://gospeltangents.com/2017/11/10/nothing-lds-theology-justifies-whacking-infants/

093: Greg Prince on History of LDS Policy Toward Gays
https://gospeltangents.com/2017/11/08/greg-prince-on-history-of-lds-policy-toward-gays/

Anne Wilde on How Polygamist Feel About Gay Marriage

Anne Wilde, founder of Principle Voices, modern-day Polygamy expert

092: How Do Polygamists Feel about Gay Marriage?
https://gospeltangents.com/2017/11/04/how-do-polygamists-feel-about-gay-marriage/

Bill Smith on Gay Marriage and D&C 132

Dr. Bill Smith, Author, *Textual Studies on the Doctrine & Covenants: The Plural Marriage Revelation.*

141: How 132 Would Affect Future Revelation on Gays & Women
https://gospeltangents.com/2018/03/31/how-132-affects-future-revelation-women-gays/

Final Note

You can get our transcripts at our amazon.com author page. I've got a link here, but just do a search for Gospel Tangents interview, and you should be able to find a bunch of them there. Please subscribe at Patreon.com/gospeltangents. For $5 a month, you can hear the entire interview uncut and for $10 you can get a pdf copy. We've also got a $15 tier where if you want a physical copy, I'll be the first to send it to you, so please subscribe at Patreon or on our website at Gospeltangents.com. For our latest updates, please like our page at facebook.com/Gospeltangents and also check our twitter updates Gospel tangents. Please subscribe on our apple podcast page tinyurl.com/GospelTangents, or you can subscribe on your android device. Just do a search for Gospel Tangents. Thanks again for listening. Click here to subscribe, here for transcript and over here we've got some more of our great videos. Thanks again.